girls who
code

Crack the Code!

Activities, Games, and Puzzles That Reveal the World of Coding

by Sarah Hutt

illustrated by Brenna Vaughan

Penguin Workshop
An Imprint of Penguin Random House

This activity book belongs to:

_____

PENGUIN WORKSHOP
Penguin Young Readers Group
An Imprint of Penguin Random House LLC

Photo credits: page 4: (portrait frames) frimages/iStock/Thinkstock; page 8: (left robot) Kirillm/iStock/Thinkstock, (center robot) Andy Crawford/Thinkstock, (right robot) Brand X Pictures/Stockbyte/Thinkstock; page 9: (robot arms) PhonlamaiPhoto/iStock/Thinkstock; page 10: Mars rover rendering courtesy of NASA; page 11: (manufacturing robot) bugphai/iStock/Thinkstock, (diving robot) JackF/iStock/Thinkstock, (dog robot) Lai leng Yiap/Hemera/Thinkstock; page 12: (toy robot) Kirillm/iStock/Thinkstock, (robot companion) EgudinKa/iStock/Thinkstock, (manufacturing robot) Thossaphoi/iStock/Thinkstock, (diving robot) JackF/iStock/Thinkstock; page 25: (manufacturing robots) PhonlamaiPhoto/iStock/Thinkstock; page 32: (laptop) Rost-9D/iStock/Thinkstock, (camera) seen0001/iStock/Thinkstock, (paint tube) Anterovium/iStock/Thinkstock, (clay) evp82/iStock/Thinkstock, (pencil) antomanio/iStock/Thinkstock, (palette) Krasyuk/iStock/Thinkstock, (paintbrush) VvoeVale/iStock/Thinkstock, (chalk) vav63/iStock/Thinkstock; page 38: (nautilus shell) joingate/iStock/Thinkstock, (roses) Vitalina/iStock/Thinkstock; page 42: (apples) CQYoung/iStock/Thinkstock; page 56: (helmet) Willard/iStock/Thinkstock, (surfboard) Purestock/Thinkstock, (T-shirt) Howard Shooter/Thinkstock; page 60: (skateboard) Ljupco/iStock/Thinkstock, (football) EHStock/iStock/Thinkstock; page 61: (athletic shoes) Tuned_In/iStock/Thinkstock, (watch) Grassetto/iStock/Thinkstock, (ski goggles) zimindmitry/iStock/Thinkstock, (baseball mitt) anopdesignstock/iStock/Thinkstock; page 85: (stage lights) Bibigon/iStock/Thinkstock; page 104: (hands logo) Anastasiia_New/iStock/Thinkstock, (cat logo) AVicons/iStock/Thinkstock, (cloud logo) Tanya-stock/iStock/Thinkstock, (scales logo) AVicons/iStock/Thinkstock; page 106: (windmill) 7Michael/iStock/Thinkstock, (vegetables) Medioimages/Photodisc/Thinkstock, (gender sign) HS3RUS/iStock/Thinkstock; page 113: (house logo) da-vooda/iStock/Thinkstock, (dog logo) nidwlw/iStock/Thinkstock, (globe logo) dikobraziy/iStock/Thinkstock.

ISBN 9780399542565   10 9 8 7 6 5 4 3 2 1

Hi, I'm Reshma, the founder of Girls Who Code. My organization teaches middle- and high-school girls how to explore their passions by writing code and creating digital games, apps, websites, and more.

Did you know that computer coding is all around you? It's used in your favorite apps and computer games, and it's also part of the latest TV shows, musical performances, athletic gear, and more.

In this book, BFFs Leila, Maya, Sophia, Erin, and Lucy walk you through their favorite ways to use computer science. Leila shows you the latest robots that can make toys, deliver packages, and even explore Mars. Maya reveals how coding can be used in art, animation, and all things fashion. Delve into the world of sports with Sophia and find out how coding can help you train for a big race. Explore coding in music and design a music library app with Erin. And whether you care about rescue animals, exercise and nutrition, or poverty and homelessness, Lucy explains how code can be used to support social causes. The options are limitless!

In addition to being super fun, the word searches, mazes, connect-the-dots, and other activities in this book will show how accessible and far-reaching coding is. Like the thousands of girls in our programs who have been inspired to learn how to code, you might even want to start your own coding project! I hope you do, and that you'll join us at one of our free coding clubs all over the country and become part of our growing sisterhood of coders.

Happy reading—and coding!

Reshma Saujani

Reshma Saujani

MEET THE GIRLS WHO CODE

LEILA

Birthday: August 22
Likes: robotics, video games, field hockey, crafting, hanging out with her big sister

MAYA

Birthday: June 3
Likes: writing, drawing, fashion, chunky jewelry, giving advice

SOPHIA

Birthday: November 13
Likes: sports, sweatpants, babysitting, nail art, taking selfies

ERIN

Birthday: February 26
Likes: baking, theater, reading, surfing, doing silly impressions

LUCY

Birthday: May 20
Likes: science, music, gardening, emojis, trying new things

In case you don't know what coding is, it's writing commands in a programming language to get a computer or digital device to do anything you dream up.

But it's not the same as just using apps or programs already installed on a computer—coding is actually *designing* the instructions to run those apps (or robots or video games).

Or to light up sound machines—or to program pretty much anything you can invent that needs a computer to make it work!

And here's something you should know about coding new inventions: The coding part is just one step in something called a **design build process**.

It looks like this:

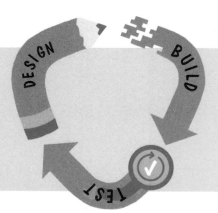

These steps are what computer scientists use to dream up, plan, build, and try out their ideas. And that's exactly what *you* can do in this book!

Totally! This book is full of doodle pages, games, and ideas about coding for robotics, music, art, animation, and to help others. And, best of all, you can do it with your friends!

(PS: You should have a pen or a pencil handy to do the activities in this book. And you can refer to the answer key at the back of the book in case you get stuck. If you need anything else, like scissors or a glue stick, we'll let you know at the top of the page.)

ALL ABOUT ROBOTS

Hi, I'm Leila! I've been fascinated by robots since I was little. Did you know that people use robots to do all sorts of things, like deliver packages, vacuum their houses, and even perform some of the jobs of astronauts in space? Robots can do so much, like move, pick stuff up, and even dance. Their ability to put things into motion is called **actuation,** and it's what makes robots different from other kinds of computers. Pretty cool, right?

If you could create any kind of robot, what would it look like? Draw it here.

What can your robot do?

clean, play, teach, help out, solve family problems, go to the grocery store, and take care of us.

Why did you make it? To help solve a problem, to address a need, or just because it's cool?

to help solve ploblems, to address a need and because its cool and more.

What are its identifying features? What do they do?

hearts, rain bows and more.

Write more about your robot.

it is kind it is a working robot and its very helpful with cleaning, playing and talking.

7

ROBOTS
OF THE
PAST

All robots are programmable machines that can perform complicated tasks on their own—like making candy or building cars in factories, filling prescriptions in pharmacies, and even farming the land.

But before robots were a reality, people had all kinds of ideas about what robots would be like in the future and what they would do—like take over the world!

Some of these are a little far-fetched, but not by that much. Today's real robots can do amazing things!

Color in and complete this super-robot comic showing what people in the past imagined robots of the future would do. Use your weirdest colors!

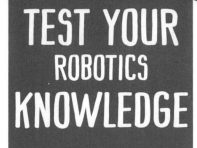

Ready to check your robotics knowledge? Answer the questions below, and see if you can separate robot fact from fiction

TRUE OR FALSE?

1. The word *robot* comes from the Slavic word *robota*, which means "forced labor," and was created by a Czech playwright in 1921.

TRUE · **FALSE**

2. Scientists have created the first robot with human feelings. It can fall in love, feel sadness, and occasionally get really mad.

TRUE · FALSE

3. Scientists and engineers have created an artificial robotic arm that can play the drums and even come up with its own beats.

TRUE · FALSE

4. It is believed that the first robot was created in 350 BC by an ancient Greek scholar. It was a mechanical air-powered bird.

TRUE · **FALSE**

5. One of the most recent inventions in robotics is a robot powered entirely by cheese. It's called ChedARbot.

TRUE · **FALSE**

6. Today, researchers are working on robots that can heal and adapt after an injury the same way animals can.

TRUE · FALSE

9

ROBOTS TODAY

Find ten differences between these two pictures of an out-of-this-world real-life robot.

This is one of two twin robots, Spirit and Odyssey. Can you guess what they're used for?

A. Making toys
B. Delivering packages
C. Exploring Mars
D. Racing other robots

It looks like it'd be great for exploring extreme alien terrain, like my brother's room when he hasn't cleaned it!

Robots can do all kinds of tasks. They're particularly well suited for jobs that are too dangerous or repetitive for humans. Take a look at the robots below, and answer the questions about them.

There are **manufacturing robots**, used to make products like cars.

Can you think of other ways robots would be helpful in manufacturing? What other products can they make?

pacaging, fac toys and more

There are **exploration robots**, used in environments too extreme for humans to survive in, such as the arctic, deep undersea, or outer space.

Why do you think scientists created a robot like this? Why can't the job be done by humans?

i think ∧ because the JOBS need to be Done fast

There are **helper robots**, used to help people with everyday tasks, like cooking, serving food, and cleaning—sometimes even to provide entertainment and company!

If you could have a robot companion, what kind would you like? What would it do?

Draw a line to match the robot to the correct job description.

A.

1. This robot has a special welding tool (something that fuses two parts together) attached to its arm for connecting machine parts.

B.

2. This deep-sea robot is specially designed to withstand frigid temperatures and dark waters so that it can explore underneath the arctic ice shelf.

C.

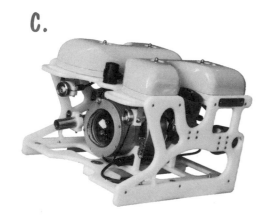

3. This robot makes going to the doctor less scary and more fun. It can keep young patients busy while doctors perform procedures.

Now that you know about all kinds of different robots, draw a robot you'd like to invent that can do something humans can't do (or that can do something better than humans). Maybe it's something in a factory, on a farm, or in your own home!

Describe its main features:

_____

_____

_____

_____

_____

_____

_____

_____

_____

_____

ROBOTS > HUMANS?

ROBOT PARTS WORD SEARCH

Because robots are a unique kind of digital device, they have some distinctive features. Learn about some important robot parts below, and then find the terms in the word search on the next page.

SENSORS:
Sensors enable robots to collect information about their setting. Just as our senses allow humans to hear, see, or feel our surroundings, sensors are the digital version for robots. There are different kinds of sensors: cameras let the robot see, microphones pick up sound, some sensors register light, and others can "feel" temperature or pressure changes.

CONTROLLER:
This is the computer inside the robot and functions as its brain. It's how you communicate with the robot—by programming it and giving it commands.

CIRCUIT BOARD:
Circuit boards house the controller and connections that allow a robot's controller to talk to all its other parts.

EFFECTORS:
These are the parts of the robot that actually do the work, such as mechanical arms, wheels to move around, or specialized tools. They're the tools you attach to a robot and control with your computer to make the whole thing function.

ACTUATORS:
These are the machine parts that drive the robot's motion. The simplest one is a motor. Actuators are what provide power to the effectors.

There are a few extra words (err . . . names) in there as a bonus. Can you guess who they are?

WORD BANK

Sensors   Effectors
~~Controller~~   Actuators
Circuit Board

K A M A Y T N T I X S F D P K
Y T C C Y S H J A R E H R K B
K A U T O A V K T V N Z A G L
J L Q P U S M Z A R S F O U R
P R H Y Z A P H E N O C B D D
W I V U D H T L N C R D T Q P
A U R Q Z V L O G E S Z I D Q
B I I U U O O M R T T P U V N
R Q N V R L Y S H S M B C B I
D I I T T W I K V W P X R P R
J E N G O I P A K V K A I M E
L O A L I E L I G C B F C M U
C Z W R W E F F E C T O R S Z
H F G D B N Q H D C R E U N Q
T S X H R P N W A U R L H F Y

IDEA LAB: ROBOT BRAINSTORM

This is Simon, my Simon Says game robot. You know that game where you have to follow a command, but you only do it if "Simon says"? I'm creating a robot that can play Simon Says. So far, I can ask it to spin around, back up, roll forward, play music, and dance. But only if Simon says!
Can you think of any other commands I could ask it to do?

It's your turn! Think back to the robot you drew on page 13. Now that you know a bit more about robots, would you still make the same kind of robot? Why or why not?

If you would make the same robot, would you change anything? What, and why? Draw your new and improved design.

What do you think you'd need to build a robot like this? Can you list some of the parts?

_____

_____

_____

_____

CIRCUIT BOARD MAZE

You already know that a circuit board is an important part of any robot. See if you can navigate your way through this one!

START

FINISH

What you'll need: scissors and glue or tape.

So far, you've been doing a lot of great thinking about what kind of robot you could make. Now it's time to make a prototype. That's when you come up with a design and then build a model or sample of the design to see how it might work. You won't be able to make a prototype of an actual working robot using this book, but for now, try cutting out the robot body you like.

Cut out the robot's parts on this page and the next page. Then get some tape or glue, and build your design prototype!

Share your work—we want to see what you made! Post it on our Facebook page, or on Twitter @girlswhocode. Be sure to ask a parent or guardian for help.

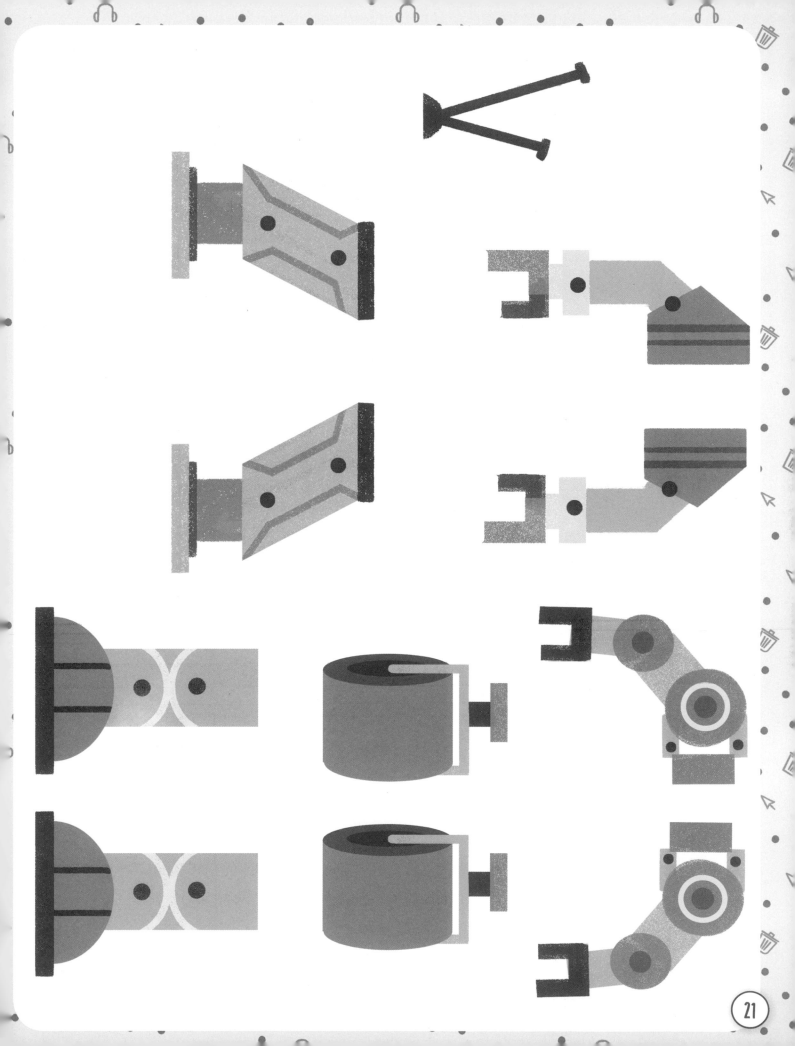

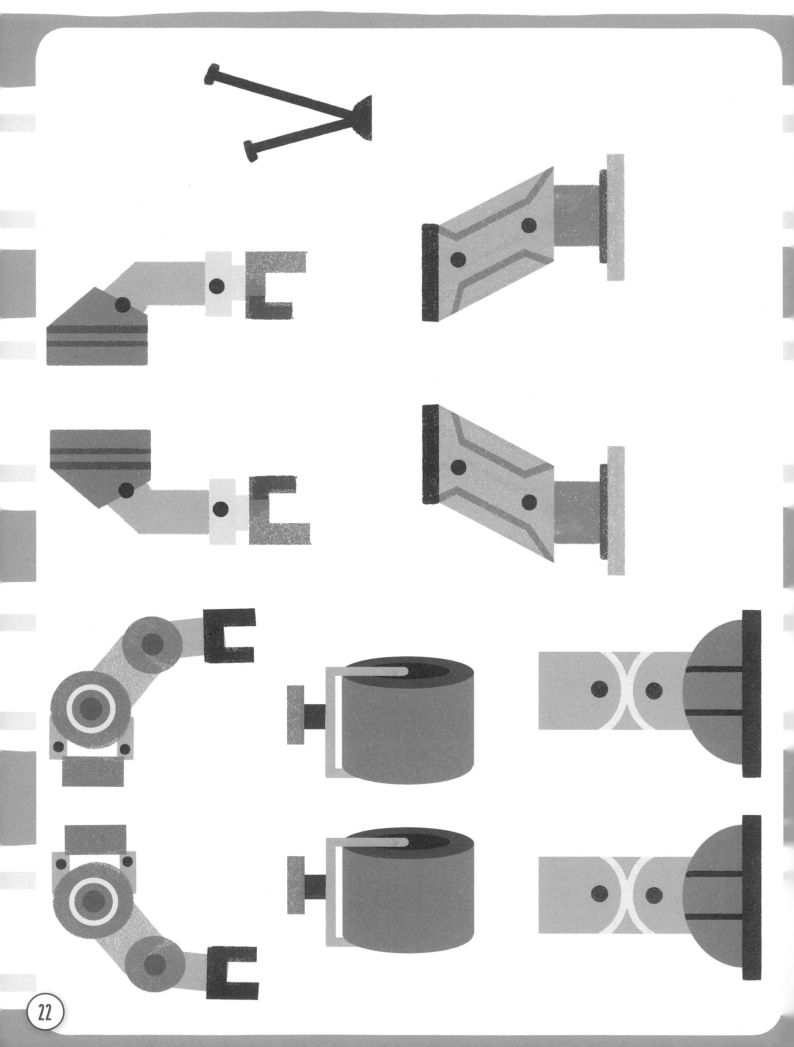

Conditionals are elements of code where one thing happens only if something else happens. Conditionals are also called **if statements**, because "if" something is true, then another thing will happen.

For example, if I finish my homework, I get to watch TV. TV watching can't happen until the condition (if my homework is done) is true.

This is an important idea in coding because it's up to you—the programmer, or person writing the code—to be as clear as possible when you write instructions for your computer.

Still not sure what this means? Play the game below to see conditionals at work.

What you'll need: a friend!
Read the sentences below out loud, and fill in the blanks so that your friend has to do each thing.

If you are wearing _____ , jump up and down on one
COLOR

foot, then spin around _____ times.
NUMBER

If you were born in _____ , sing "Happy Birthday" at
MONTH

the top of your lungs, then take a bow.

If you love _____ , do your best impression of
NAME OF FAVORITE
MUSICIAN/POP STAR
him/her.

Where do you think this robot is? Use your imagination to complete the scene. Add any features you want to the robot to make it better!

Here's a hint: These robots are used in manufacturing to make something a lot of people use to get around in.

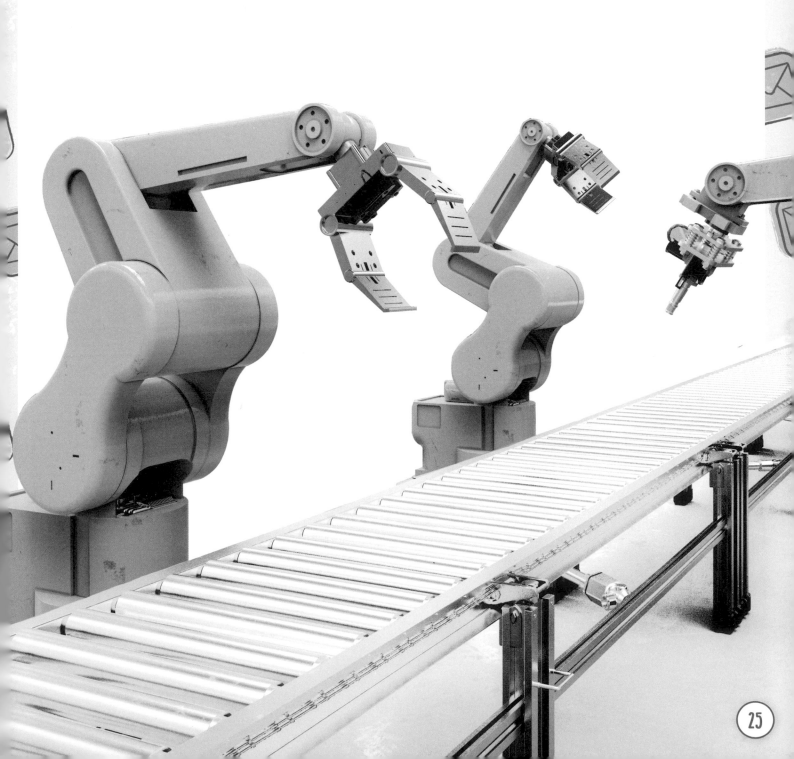

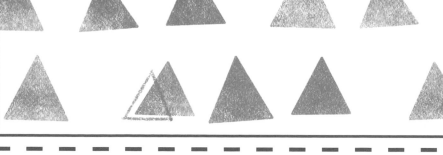

MAKE IT BETTER: CONDITIONAL NAVIGATION GAME

What you'll need: scissors, removable tape, and a friend!

After you've worked through the **design build cycle**, there's an important next step that you can always do—make it better! Once you've tested your project, it's always a good idea to think about how it worked, what you've learned, and how you can make your ideas, designs, and prototypes even better. This card game is a chance for you to do just that, and to improve on an idea you've already thought of.

Remember the conditionals word game on page 23? Take what you learned from it, and turn it into a real-life obstacle course! Cut out the **If/Then** cards on the next page and use them to make a maze in a room where you're going to play this game—maybe your bedroom or living room, for example.

Use chairs, pillows, or anything else you can find to create obstacles. Get some tape and hang up the cards in key places in the room, with the correct command written in pencil.

Another player has to follow the instructions, and can only do the exact instructions to get from one card to the next in order to complete the maze.

For example, If (you reach the couch, take two steps to the right), then (walk four steps forward). Feel free to change and improve your instructions to get your friend through the obstacle course!

IF _____   THEN _____

IF _____   THEN _____

IF _____   THEN _____

IF _____   THEN _____

IF _____   THEN _____

IF _____   THEN _____

START   FINISH

IF _____   THEN _____

IF _____   THEN _____

IF _____   THEN _____

IF _____   THEN _____

IF _____   THEN _____

IF _____   THEN _____

START   FINISH

Let's talk about the game you just played. What worked? What didn't? What was the funniest moment when everything went wrong?

What was the coolest part, where things seemed to work just right?

What can you do to make it better next time? Would you change the instructions on the game? Modify the cards? Make more or fewer cards? Change your instructions?

How can the ideas and concepts you've explored apply to how you might program a robot to move through an obstacle course?

Congratulations! You just worked through a whole **design build cycle** on the topic of robots! Ready for something new?

ALL ABOUT: DIGITAL ART AND ANIMATION

I'm Maya. I love drawing, writing, and all things fashion—I even like to sew my own clothes! One of my favorite things to do is to go through my art or sewing box to find just the right paint, crayon, thread, or fabric to bring a new idea to life. The cool thing about coding is that it's not that different from art—it's just another way I can create anything I dream up!

What kinds of things do you like to create, and what are your favorite tools for creating them? Write about or draw them here.

Draw a picture of your favorite creative tool and something you've made with it. (If your favorite creative tool is an art supply, use it to draw your picture!)

Why is this your favorite tool?
What do you like to make with it?
How do you think you could use code to build/expand on this creation?

_____

_____

_____

_____

_____

_____

_____

_____

_____

ARTSY CRAFTSY

When you think about art, you might picture old paintings hanging in gold frames in a museum. But there are so many different types of art—there's sculpture, photography, installation art, audiovisual art, animation, illustration, crafts, textiles, woodworking, and so much more. Coding can be yet another great way to express yourself visually.

Use the images below to find the answers to this crossword puzzle. Each clue is some kind of artistic tool.

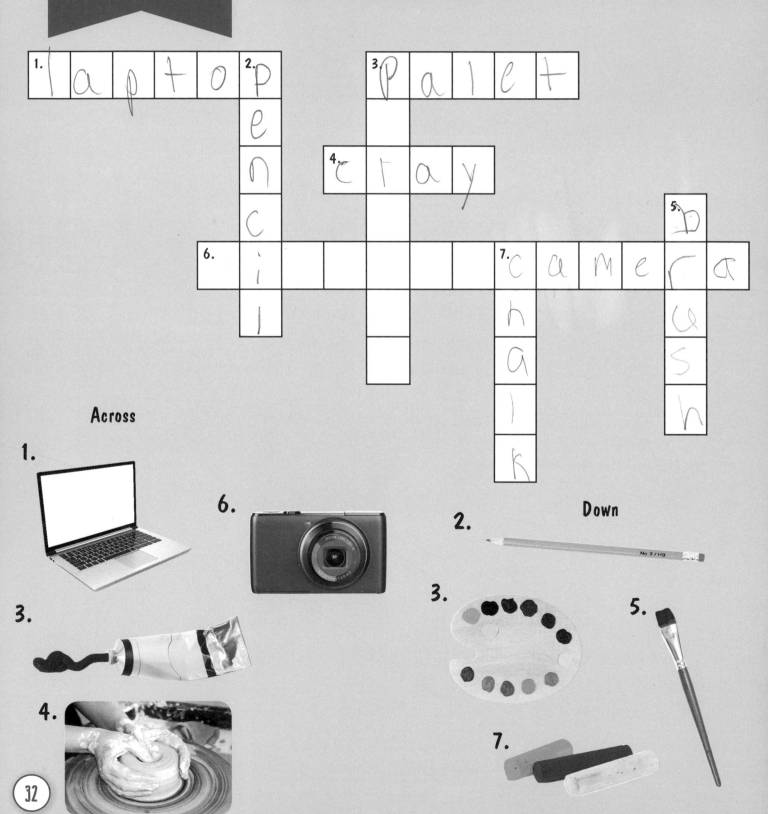

1. laptop
2. pencil
3. palet
4. cray
5. b
6. (blank)
7. camera
chair
rush (brush)

Across

1.

6.

3.

4.

Down

2.

3.

5.

7.

When you use coding to make art, you may not be dipping a brush in paint or drawing with a colored pencil. But you *can* create pictures using digital pens, or take pictures with a digital camera and code a program to animate them. You can also use code to make lots of shapes, spirals, and designs that automatically appear. This is called **generative art**. And you can even create interactive installations—like light shows—that audiences can engage with!

Think of five ways in which computers, coding, or any kind of digital device could help you create art. You could use music, light, cameras, digital drawings, or anything else to create your masterpiece.

List and describe them here.

1. _____

   _____

2. _____

   _____

3. _____

   _____

4. _____

   _____

5. _____

   _____

You just learned that there are many ways you can use coding to create art. Here are some clues to help you find out more. Connect the dots on the next page to find out the right answers.

1. This device lets you edit digital images to bring them to life as movies. What is it?

_____

2. This device lets you capture digital images, which you can then modify and design using code. What is it?

_____

3. These devices lets you draw, paint, and sketch straight into your computer. What is it?

_____

1.

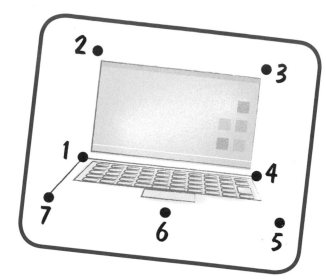

2.

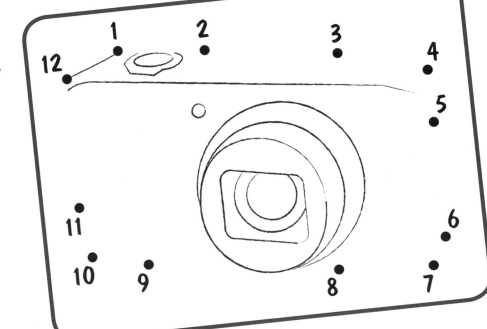

3.

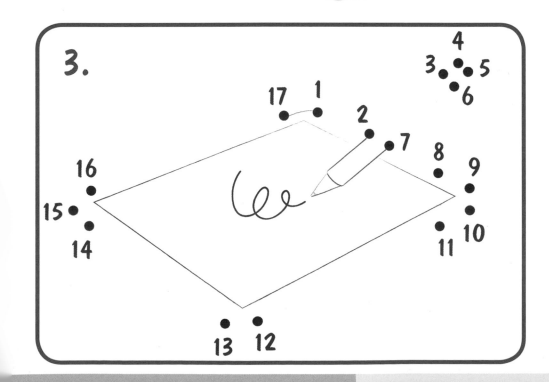

IDEA LAB: COLLAGE

One of my favorite art projects is to make collages. I love collages because you can take ideas and inspiration from everywhere—books, magazines, words on a page, icons, colors . . . anything, really! Then you blend them all together to create something new and exciting.

When you're coming up with a new idea for a digital product or coding project, collages are a great way to brainstorm ideas. It can help you figure out what is useful and interesting to the person who will use that product and how they will use it. This is called **user experience**, or **UX**.

I'm working on a website to sell my craft accessories. Can you help me figure out which colors, style, and layout I should use to make it easy for customers to find and buy my crafts?

Here are a few of the items I'd like to display:
- Hand-knitted winter hats and gloves
- Beaded dangle earrings
- Woven friendship bracelets

What you'll need: scissors, a glue stick, old magazines, and colored pencils, crayons, or markers.

I'd love your help coming up with a design for my site. See if you can find colors that complement my products. You could check out some cool websites for custom jewelry and crafts to get ideas. Cut out images from magazines and paste the images you like. Experiment with text or fonts you like, too. Try to pick things that go together well in an interesting or artistic way. Your collage will be the inspiration for my website!

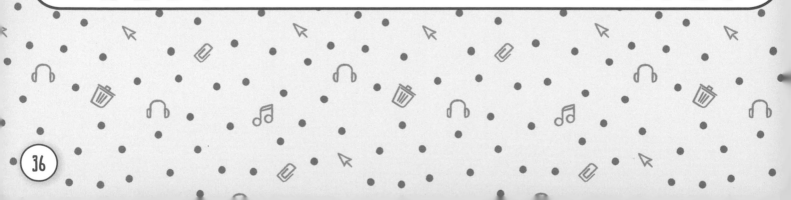

GENERATIVE ART: SPIRALS

Coding is a great way to create and generate cool shapes, patterns, and spirals. By coming up with just the right algorithm (a set of instructions written in code that your computer can follow), your code can generate all kinds of amazing artwork. This type of digital design is a form of **generative art**. But before you can code a pattern or design, you have to map it out to figure out the right sequence.

The pattern on this page is called the Fibonacci or Golden Spiral. It's the representation of a magical number sequence that appears in nature repeatedly, such as the spiral of a snail shell or an open rose.

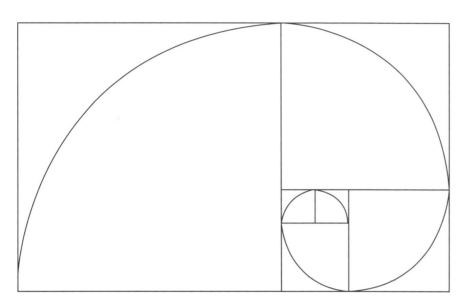

The sequence is special because every number after the first two are the sum of the two numbers before it. It looks like this: 1, 1, 2, 3, 5, 8, 13, and so on.

Now you can complete the Fibonacci Spiral! Follow the steps below in the algorithm and see if you can complete the pattern.

Before you do, you may want to practice connecting one corner of each square with the other using a slow curving line like the one on the previous page.

Here are some practice squares.
Ready?

1. Put your pencil or pen in the lower right-hand corner of the #1 square. It's noted with a little star.
2. Draw a curved line to the opposite corner.
3. Now you're in the next #1 box. Continue to draw your curved line to the opposite corner of that box, until you reach the corner of the #2 box.
4. Continue to draw a curved line to the opposite corner of each remaining box.

Good job! That's how you generate a Golden Spiral.

OPTICAL ILLUSIONS

Another fun thing to do with code is to create optical illusions. An image can be animated using code to make the illusion appear, but first you have to understand how it works.

What you'll need: colored pencils, crayons, or markers.

Pick three colors and assign each one a number value: 0, 1, or 2. Now color in the grid using your color code.

Oooh, I like this. I want to make a costume with that cool pattern!

Color 0   Color 1   Color 2

Now it's your turn! Try your hand at drawing and color-coding your own optical illusion. Need some inspiration? You can always do some research. Look up "optical illusions" online and see what comes up. Use what you find to inspire you to make your own unique creation.

3-D PRINTING BONANZA!

You already know you can use computers to make digital drawings, create generative art, and take pictures. But did you know that you can make real-life sculptures using a digital device? It's called a 3-D printer. Instead of using ink to print, this printer uses a liquid medium that hardens when it dries—such as thin plastic, metal, clay, or even chocolate!—to print three-dimensional objects. That means objects with height, width, and depth. For example, a chunky bracelet or a sculpture.

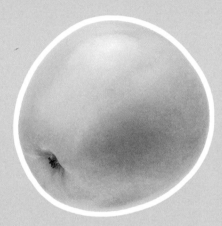

This is what an apple looks like in 2-D, which basically means *flat*.

Here's what an apple looks like from the side and from an angle when we try to represent it in 3-D.

Now imagine if you took a real apple and sliced it across the middle, into tiny thin slices top to bottom. By themselves they are just thin slices, but if you stacked them up in the right order, they would take the shape of the apple. That's exactly what 3-D printing does.

To create 3-D printing, special software takes all the dimensions—height, width, and depth—for every part of the three-dimensional object you want to print and then calculates how to break that object down into lots and lots of super-thin slices.

The 3-D printer then prints those slices stacked one by one on top of each other to create a real-life three-dimensional object. Pretty amazing, right?

Now take some 2-D objects and turn them into 3-D ones by following the directions. Color them in when you are done!

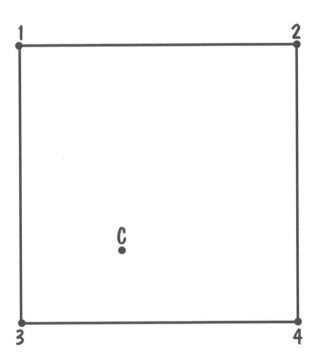

A

B

TO TURN THE SQUARE INTO A CUBE:

1. Draw a line from point 1 to point A.
2. Draw a line from point 2 to point B.
3. Draw a line from point 3 to point C.
4. Draw a line from point 4 to point D.
5. Draw a line from point A to point B.
6. Draw a line from point B to point D.
7. Draw a line from point C to point D.
8. Draw a line from point A to point C.

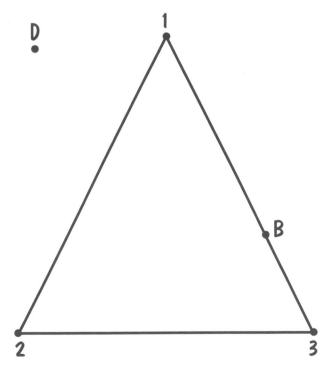

D

TO TURN THE TRIANGLE INTO A PYRAMID:

A•

1. Draw a line from point 1 to point A.
2. Draw a line from point A to point 2.
3. Draw a line from point A to point B.

Next, see if you can turn your 3-D shapes into something else, like a house or ice cream. Be creative!

ANIMATE THIS!

What you'll need: scissors, a pen, a stapler, and staples.

One of the best-known forms of digital art is animation. Do you watch Saturday-morning cartoons, animated movies at the theater, or animated stop-motion videos online? They're all made through digital animation. From the original art to the actual animating (which means creating the illusion of movement), almost all of modern animation is done with computers.

We'll let you in on a secret: Animation is actually an illusion. Whether it's digital or drawn by hand, all animation is just a series of images, one after another, that are each changed just a bit in order to create a sense of movement. Crazy, huh?

Yup! And the simplest form of animation out there is a flip book. Want to see for yourself?

Cut out the cards on the next page. Put all the cards with the shooting star on them facing up, and stack them in numbered order, with number one at the top of the stack. Then staple them together. There are smaller stars on the first card to show you where to staple them.

Notice how the star is in a slightly different place on each page? Remember that.

Now hold the book in one hand, put your thumb at the bottom corner, bend the book a little, and let the pages out from under your thumb one at a time. Look at the shooting star!

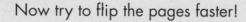
Now try to flip the pages faster!

You can even create a flip book yourself. Flip the book over and draw a stick figure waving or walking on a sunny day. Remember to make each picture just a little different by moving the position of the waving hand from one side to the other on each page. Then flip through, and see your stick figure come alive!

4.

8.

12.

16.

20.

3.

7.

11.

15.

19.

2.

6.

10.

14.

18.

1. ★ ★

5.

9.

13.

17.

45

Design your own emojis to describe how you feel right now. You can make one to show how you feel about coding—excited, interested, nervous, or maybe somewhere in between? What about the activities in the book—how do they make you feel? Make an emoji about your favorite activity.

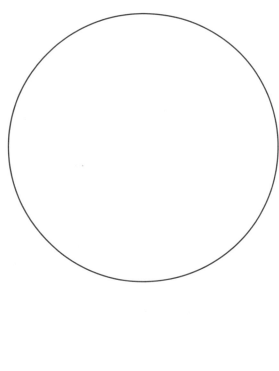

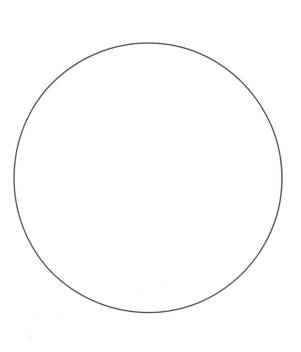

MAKE IT BETTER: ALGORITHM GAME

You know that an algorithm is a set of instructions that tell your computer how to do something. But did you know that algorithms aren't something only computers can understand? Any set of instructions is an algorithm.

Totally. Below is an algorithm game to show you what we mean. Here's how it goes.

Find a friend to be your partner. Then, on a separate piece of paper, draw something without showing your partner. It can be something really simple, like a square, or a more complicated doodle.

Now here's the tricky part. You have to explain, step by step, how to draw the same thing, using only words. Write the instructions down here. Your partner will then try drawing it on the opposite page.

Have your friend create a drawing here,
based on your instructions.

How did you do? Once you're done, revisit the instructions you came up with, and look for places to improve the instructions to make your drawings match. Can you make your algorithms better? Here's room to write out your improved algorithm.

By now I bet you're feeling super inspired to try coding for art. Just in case you still don't know what to make, here's a fortune-teller game full of fun ideas for creative coding projects. Use it to help you figure out what to design, who your project is for, and what it should do. This fortune-teller won't give you all the answers, but it'll help you generate your best ideas. So let's get started!

Follow the directions on the next page to make the game.

CIRCLE

TRIANGLE

Do you want your design to meet a need?

Do you want your design to be for a certain type of user?

Create a comic strip you can animate to tell a story.

Do you want your design to replace something that already exists?

Do you want your design to be silly and funky?

Plan a design for a 3-D printed sculpture.

Write code to generate an animated screen saver.

Do you want your design to take a long time to make?

Make a collage of digital images to help you figure out an idea.

Do you want your design to be practical with no frills?

SQUARE

DIAMOND

Do you want your design to inspire?

Do you want your design to educate?

FORTUNE-TELLER

What you'll need: scissors, a pen, paper, and a friend!

FORTUNE-TELLER INSTRUCTIONS

1. Cut out the fortune-teller page from this book.
2. Place it facedown.
3. Fold each corner into the center of the square.
4. Flip the fortune-teller over.
5. Fold each corner into the center of the square again.
6. Put your fingers in the corner flaps of the fortune-teller, and start telling fortunes!

HOW TO PLAY

Once you've folded your fortune-teller, find a friend. (The game also works on your own!) One of you inserts your fingers into the flaps to move the fortune-teller. The other picks a shape. Spell the word out loud as you flip the fortune-teller back and forth for each letter. When you get to the end of the word, choose the next flap to open. You'll see a question. Think about it, and then spell out your answer (yes or no) as you move the flaps. When you stop, open the flap for a suggestion. Now comes the fun part—think about the question you answered and the design suggestion you got. Write it down, and you can start working on it later! Now try playing the fortune-teller again, or have your friend give it a try!

CODING AND SPORTS

Hey, what's up? I'm Sophia, and I'm *totally* into sports. I never paid much attention to coding. I mean, there are no sprints, passes, high jumps, or complicated plays to figure out in coding, right? Turns out I was wrong! When I started getting into computer science, I came up with all sorts of awesome ways to use coding to help me track my times, measure my jumps, work out complicated plays—and, of course, build a totally amazing fan page for my favorite team. And the coolest thing is that coding is kind of like sports: They both require creativity, precision, attention to detail, and a whole lot of practice to get better. Which makes coding my kind of challenge!

What are your favorite sports or games?

Draw a picture of one of your favorite sports.
Do you like to play this sport or just watch it?

How do you think coding could help you enjoy your favorite sport
even more? Draw your idea.

SPORTS CODE

There are lots of ways computers can be used in sports—and not just on the field. Coding can help fans track their favorite teams and check their stats, and athletes can improve their performance by keeping track of how they're doing through apps and other digital programs. Coding can even help everyone play safer when they're enjoying their favorite sports!

Here is some common sports gear that has been improved (or that people are trying to improve) with coding. Write what the item is, and read about its digital version.

_____

High-tech versions of this item could help protect players from concussions.

_____

Having a digital prototype of this item means it could more easily be reconstructed if it broke.

_____

Digital versions of this item could adjust to its wearer's temperature.

Add your idea for a digital sporting product to the appropriate column. Some may overlap! Then see if you can think of some more.

EQUIPMENT/ GEAR	TRAINING/ PRACTICING	WATCHING/ SUPPORTING

TEAM NAME GENERATOR

Computers are good at generating lots of random numbers or word combinations. Usually, this kind of algorithm is used to come up with super-secure passwords. But let's use the idea to have some fun and generate a random name for our school sports team!

What you'll need: a friend!

Have your friend call out a letter from A to J and a number from 1 to 10 at random. Then check their combination against the list below, and tell them their team name! Try it a few times and see how silly the names can get.

A	Flying	1	Penguins
B	Running	2	Falcons
C	Fighting	3	Bananas
D	Amazing	4	Laptops
E	Battling	5	Manatees
F	Super	6	Code Stars
G	Sonic	7	Cheetahs
H	All-Star	8	Jellyfish
I	Incredible	9	Lions
J	Digital	10	Ducks

When you come up with your favorite team name, draw a team logo, jersey, and name banner for your team!

IDEA LAB: WHAT CAN YOU CODE?

Now that you've seen a few ways that coding and digital technology can be used in sports, it's your turn to brainstorm. Take a look at the basic sports equipment below. How do you think you could make each one of these items better with coding? What features could you add? Maybe a camera on the skateboard, or lights built into the ski goggles?

Draw them in, and then annotate your design. That means draw a line to a new feature, and write an explanation describing what you've added and how it will improve the item.

SKATEBOARD

FOOTBALL

ATHLETIC SHOES

WATCH

SKI GOGGLES

BASEBALL MITT

61

BATTER UP!

Connect the dots to see a smart sports product at work. Color in the page when you're done!

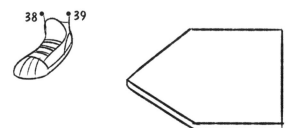

Connect the dots to see another smart sports product at work. Color in the page when you're done!

This is awesome! I can track my rides and get some backup power for a boost!

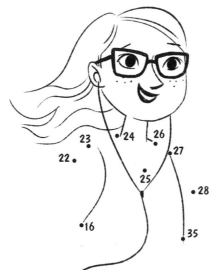

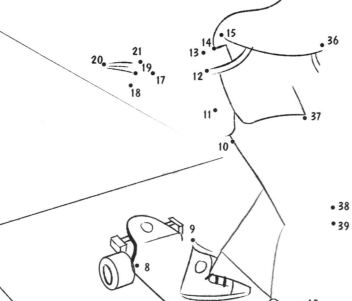
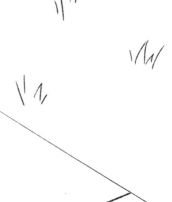

DESIGN LAB: CODE STARS

In video-game design, storyboards are a big part of mapping out how a game will flow. They're like a little comic book where you can draw what will happen in a game as you move through it.
Like this . . .

I want to create an interactive obstacle course game where players have to run, jump, and climb to collect prizes. The prizes are different coding skills. I'm calling it Code Stars!

Can you help me draw the obstacle course? You can add a rope climb, a climbing wall, hopscotch jumps, leaps—or anything else you can think of for players to go through. Ready?

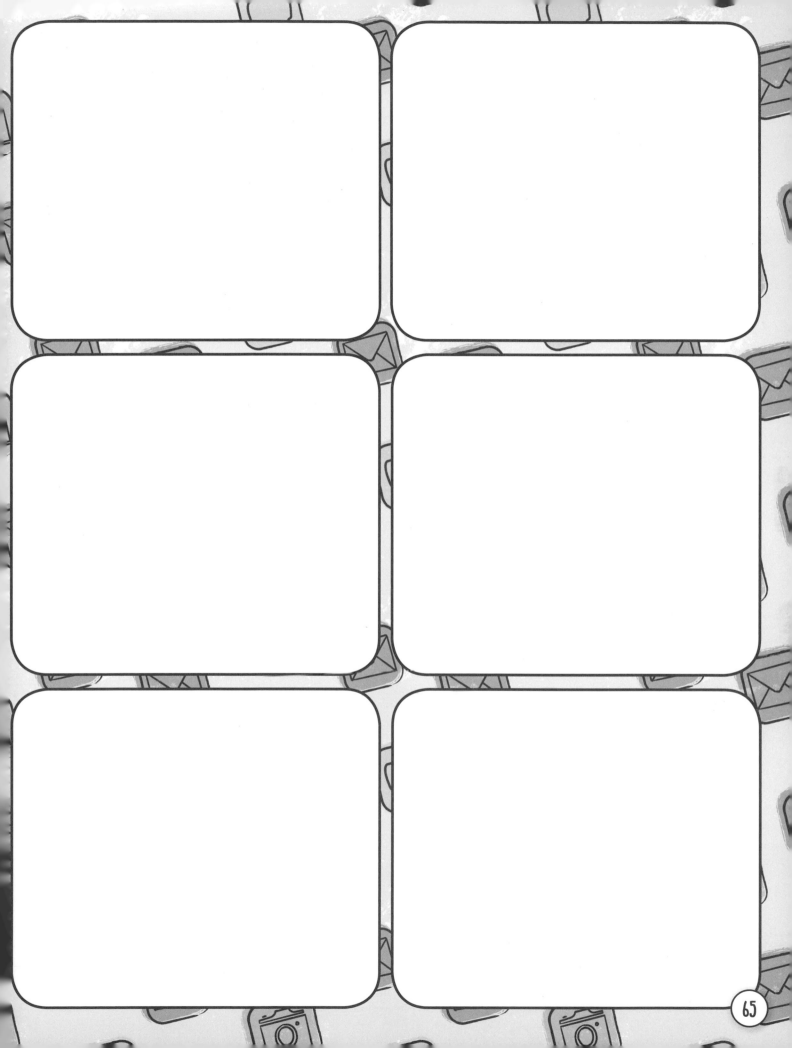

Complete this summery scene. Add anything you'd like to create a super-fun summer sports day. You can color it in, too!

Is there a coding project or a digital device that could improve what's happening in the scene you just finished drawing and coloring? Maybe an app to measure tide times and map local wave breaks, for example. Describe and draw it here.

WINTER FUN

Complete this wintry scene. Add anything you'd like to show a snowy winter sports day. You can color it in, too!

Is there some technology that could improve what's happening in the scene you just finished drawing and coloring? Maybe an app to tell how thick the snow is, for example. Describe and draw it here. If you can't think of anything that needs coding, that's okay, too. You don't always need to add tech just to add tech!

TRY IT OUT: DRILL LOOPS

In coding, a loop is a set of coded instructions that repeats until there is another instruction that makes the loop stop. A loop that goes on and on is called an **infinite loop**. The reason you create loops is to simplify the instructions for a computer, so you don't have to write repeated lines of code over and over again.

If you think about it, loops are kind of like sports drills (or an exercise routine). You repeat sports drills until you start the next exercise, right? Then a new loop starts. Just like loops in computers!

Now imagine you are writing out your drill or exercise routine. If you had to write the same thing as many times as you had to do it, it would take forever.

So instead of writing ten lines that say "touch your toes," you can write one line that says "touch your toes ten times." You could also say "shoot baskets for ten minutes," or "do pull-ups until you can't anymore."

It's a huge time-saver. Want to try it out?

On the next page, there are cards with exercise drills on them. Cut out the cards and shuffle them, and then draw one card at a time and follow the instructions. When you complete the loop on one card, draw another one and start the next loop.

Want to see an even bigger loop at work? Start the whole sequence again! And if you want to come up with your own loops, you can write them on the back of the cards.

You can make them as sporty or silly as you like. I like "hop on one leg and cluck like a chicken ten times."

1. Do ten jumping jacks.

2. Bend down and touch your toes. Count to ten, and then come up again.

3. Jump in place ten times.

4. Jog in place and count to ten. When you reach ten, stop.

5. Circle your arms ten times. Then reverse direction and circle ten more times.

6. Do ten sit-ups.

7. Spin around ten times (careful if you get dizzy!).

8. Do ten twists to your left side.

9. Do ten twists to your right side.

10. Reach your left arm over your head and side bend to the right. Repeat on the left. Go back and forth, switching sides eight more times.

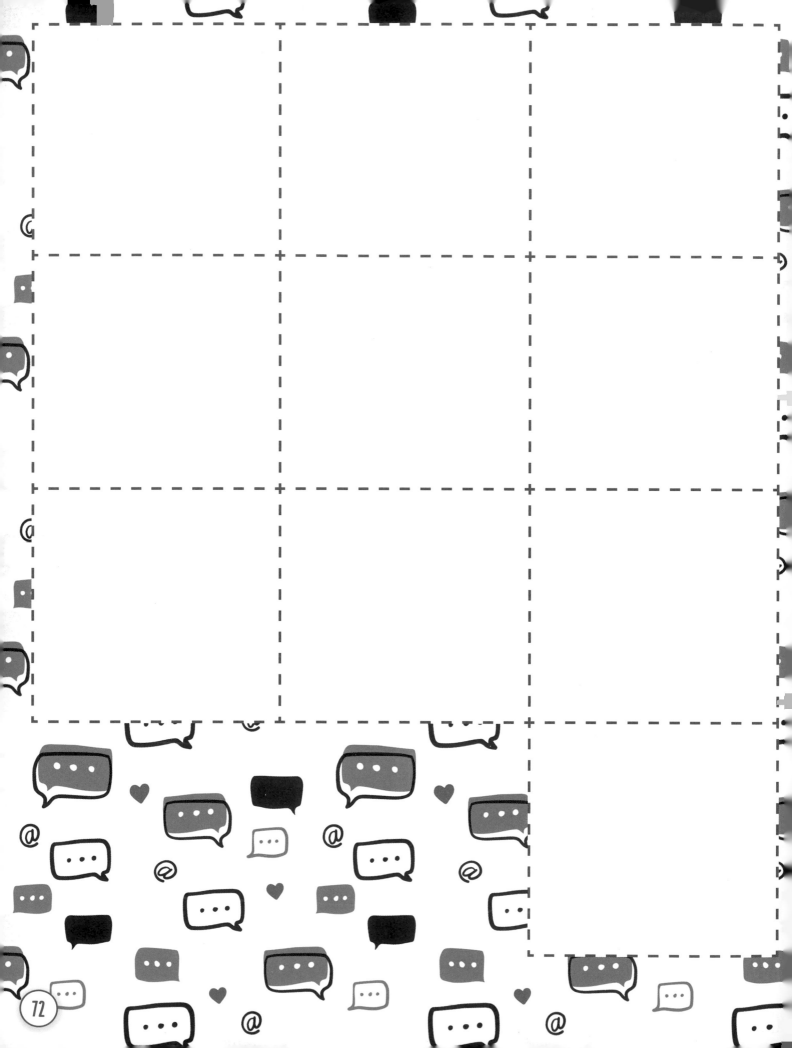

You already know computers are good at generating lots of random numbers for things like passwords and secret codes. They're also great at cracking those codes. Try to unscramble these coding- and sports-themed words to see how good *you* are at cracking the code!

Want to make it into a game? Time yourself. Then give the same game to a friend and see who gets the faster time!

CRACK THE CODE!

BALBASLE ....

BEWTISE ....

KARTC NAD DILEF ....

HOTTSWAPC ....

GLIATID CEDVIE ....

PUJM TOSH ....

TALNEPY ....

CRATEK ....

BADOWSRON ....

TELMHE CRAEMA ....

LOOPS AND BRANCHING MAZE

Remember the Code Stars video game you made the storyboards for? Imagine the same obstacle course as a series of loops and branching conditionals. Find your way out of the loops, down the right branch, and out of the maze to claim your Code Stars prize!

START

FINISH

DIGITAL DIVAS: MUSIC AND PERFORMANCE WITH CODE

Introducing the one, the only, Erin! Hi there! Are you excited about coding yet? I totally am. Oh my gosh, coding for music, theater, dance, and performance is the best! Basically, anything you can think of to make shows more interesting and fun for the audience, you can do with code!

I love singing and acting. I'm a huge fan of musicals, or anything that requires me to do accents. What about you? What are your favorite kinds of shows to perform in or to attend? Live music, dance, theater?

_____

_____

_____

_____

_____

_____

_____

_____

_____

_____

_____

_____

How do you think you could use coding for a music, dance, or theater performance? Would you use it to make the performance better, like code for amplifying an instrument or helping a musician? Or would it be something to make the show better for the audience, like code for lighting or sound design? Write and draw your ideas here!

ANALOG OR DIGITAL?

When I first started coding, I didn't totally realize what digital technology meant. I found out that it's basically anything that uses a computer to operate. And as you already know, computers work because coded instructions written by programmers tell them what to do.

But just because something uses electricity doesn't mean it's digital. It has to have some kind of computer in it to be considered digital.

Color in this vintage electric guitar with your coolest colors. It may be electric, but it's not digital!

Electrical instruments and devices that don't use computers are called analog devices.

But you know what? An instrument doesn't need to be digital to make digital music. You can record the sound of an electric guitar, capture it in a computer, and then use special software to mix and modify the sound. Pretty neat, right? It's all about how you capture and use the sound, which is why coding opens up all kinds of possibilities.

Use the space below to dream up your own digital musical device. How does the computer part of it change the sound? Is it like any instrument you've played? How is it different? Then brainstorm some facts about your new instrument below!

Name of instrument: ....

The performer who plays this instrument is called: ....

....

It sounds like: ....

....

It's digital because the computer part of it changes the sound so that:

....

....

The most famous songs that could use this instrument include: ....

....

IDEA LAB: CARD SORTING

What you'll need: scissors and a friend!

I have a huge music collection—from show tunes to pop hits to rock, hip-hop, and jazz. Some are songs I like to listen to, some I use for dance practice, and others I'm learning to play for shows and concerts.

That's why I'm working on a music library app to keep my collection organized—it's a lot to keep track of! But I want to make sure what I come up with is useful and works for the way I like to listen to music.

The problem is, it's hard to decide what features to include. And it's way too easy to add too many features, which just makes the project harder to code.

I've learned that a good way to figure out how to prioritize features—which means deciding which are the most important—is something called **card sorting**. You can use it for something you are making for yourself, but it's also a helpful way to figure out which features are most important to other users.

Want to try this design experiment yourself?

Cut out the cards on the next page. One side lists features for my music app. The other side is blank, so you can write in any features you can think of. Take your cards and sort them in order of importance. Write down your list.

Now give the cards to a friend, and have them sort the cards in order of importance to them. Do you notice any differences?

Sort by artist

Sort by song length

Sheet music for song

Tutorial videos for how to play a song

Music video for a song

Share songs library

Create custom playlists

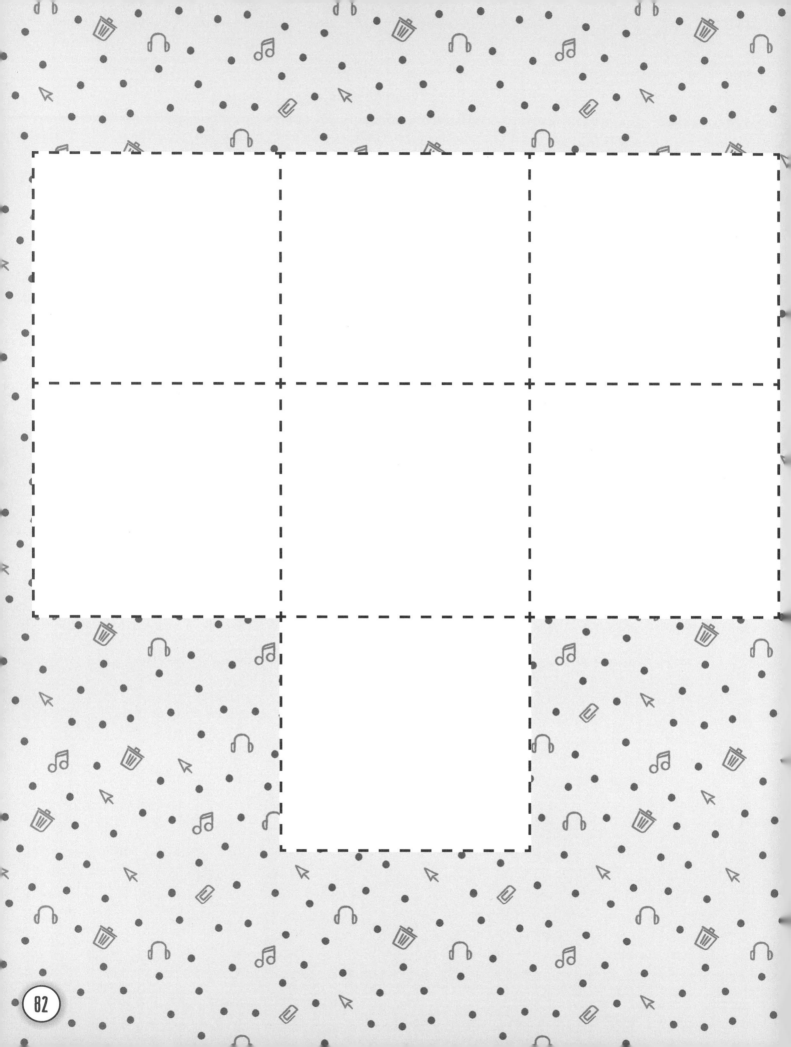

All computers do pretty much the same thing: They take input, run a process on it, and create an output. This can be as simple as inputting a series of letters on a keyboard, and outputting words into a digital document.

When you connect an instrument to a digital device, like a mix board, there are a lot of inputs and outputs to keep track of. See if you can make your way through this maze!

INPUT/OUTPUT CABLE CONNECTOR MAZE

FINISH

START

TEST

DESIGN LAB: STAGE LIGHTING

What you'll need: scissors, and colored pencils, crayons, or markers.

Have you been to a concert or performance that had an amazing light display? Lighting designers often use coding to program lights! Color in the cutouts on the next page, then cut them out and arrange them along the edges of the stage to put together a design for a lighting display. But don't glue or fasten them in place—you may want to use these lights again later!

Color in the rest of the stage to make the coolest-ever backdrop for a concert or show.

Ready to try your code-cracking skills on some music, art, and performance words? Lights, places, unscramble!

CRAPHEYHROOG ....

TGINLIGH SENDIG ....

NUSOD GIXMIN DRABO ....

NYTZEHSSIER ....

MCUTESO ....

RECODRIT ....

RETNOCC ....

MEPROFRANCE ....

SUMIC ....

HETRAET ....

ACTOR'S NIGHTMARE WORD GAME

Uh-oh, Erin forgot her lines. Fill in the word game on the next page to help her out. But first, color in the scene.

Two households, both alike in _____,
                                        NOUN

In fair _____, where we lay our _____,
          A PLACE   NOUN

From ancient _____ break to new _____,
                  NOUN   NOUN

Where _____ _____ makes _____ hands
          ADJECTIVE   NOUN   ADJECTIVE

unclean.

From forth the fatal _____ of these two _____
                          PLURAL NOUN   PLURAL NOUN

A pair of star-cross'd _____ _____ their _____ . . .
                            PLURAL NOUN   VERB   NOUN

Umm, not sure Erin wants to say that in front of an audience.

Can you think of an app that could help you memorize or practice lines to a play or words to a song? How would it work? Describe it here.

_____

_____

_____

_____

TRY IT OUT:
MAKE MUSIC
WITH
FUNCTIONS

What you'll need: scissors and a friend!

Whoa, after that actor's nightmare, I'm going to focus on making music for a bit. And there's a really easy, fun way to do that using a computer science concept called **functions**.

In computer coding, functions are short bunches of code that do specific jobs in a larger program. They're self-contained pieces, kind of like a sample or theme in a larger piece of music.

Want to test out the idea?

Cut out the cards on the next page. Find a friend, and line up the cards at random, then follow the functions' instructions to make music.

X means a quick beat.

— means a pause.

You can rearrange the cards to make your own music. Or divide them up with your friend and perform them at the same time for a duet.

Can you play an instrument, or do you want to create your own function? Write your ideas on the back of the cards, and work them into the game.

SING:
La Di Da,
Di Da

TAP:
x, x, x—x, x, x

HUM:
One long low
hum

CLAP:
x—x—x—x

SING:
Ooooh, Ooooh,
Ooooh, Ooooh

WHISTLE:
Any tune you
can think of

TAP:
x, x, x, x, x,
x, x, x

**CLAP, CLAP,
STOMP, CLAP,
CLAP, STOMP**

HUM:
High, Low,
High, Low,
High, Low,
Lower

WHISTLE:
x, x, x, x—x,
x, x, x

Awesome—we just had our first band practice! Now we need a name. I really liked Sophia's Team Name generator idea. I want to try it to generate a random name for a band. Let's do it together!

BAND NAME GENERATOR

What you'll need: a friend!

Have your friend call out a letter from A to J and a number from 1 to 10 at random. Then check their combination against the list below, and tell them their band name! Try it a few times and see how silly the names can get.

A	Amazing	1	Sneakers
B	Neon	2	Sweatpants
C	Howlin'	3	Papayas
D	Electric	4	Monkeys
E	Rockin'	5	Waves
F	Funky Funky	6	Gravy
G	Digital	7	Code Sisters
H	Space	8	Lunch Box
I	Groovy	9	Leg Warmers
J	Plastic	10	Terabyte

When you come up with your favorite band name, draw a logo and design your concert T-shirt! Do you plan to use coding to play your music, amplify your sound, and create a cool light show for your performances? Describe how you'll use coding below.

By now you might have figured out that I love to put on a show. And one of my favorite things to do is get my friends to help me design costumes for different dance numbers. Can you help out?

Draw an outfit on each character to match their dance style. Then cut them out and keep them handy—you'll be using them again soon.

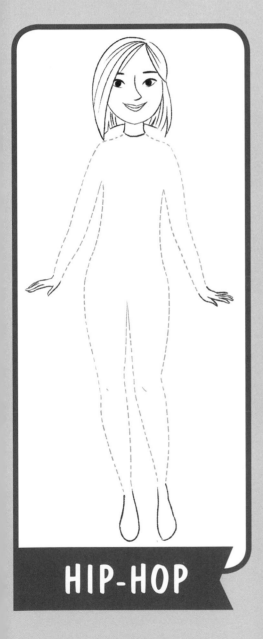

HIP-HOP

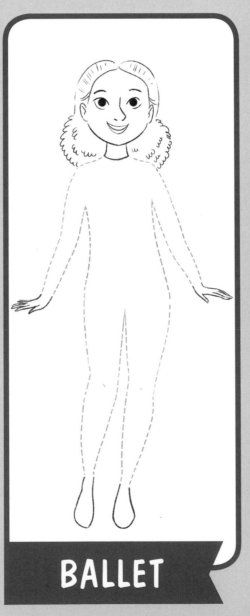

BALLET

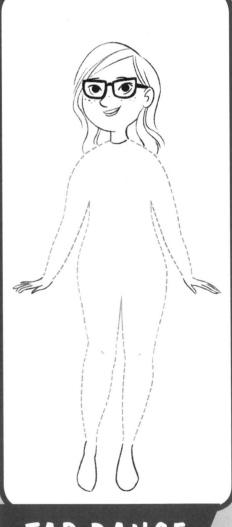

TAP DANCE

There are a lot of moving parts that go into putting on a show. You have to think about the lighting, the music, and the costumes, for example. The singers need to know their parts, the actors their lines, and the musicians their songs. Then you have to put it all together for an audience to enjoy. Sound like anything else you know about?

That's right—it's the same thing with coding! There are a lot of small pieces that need to be figured out one by one, and put together in the right order. Then, at the right time, they need to all work together and function well for a user.

Which is why a coding project—just like a complicated show—has to be carefully planned and then written out. First, color in this poster announcing the show!

Tonight, for one night only, the amazing

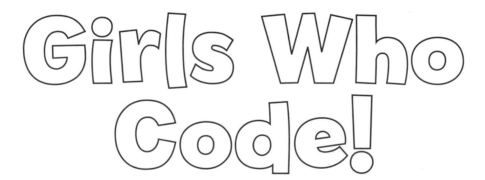

Girls Who Code!

Don't miss Erin, Maya, Lucy, Leila, and Sophia in a super-secret mystery performance!

Use this stage and your light cutouts from page 85, your character cutouts from page 95, and your music functions from page 91 to plan out a show.

Think about the order you want things to happen in. Do the lights come up first, and then the music starts? When do the dancers come out? Play around on your model. Color, cut, paste, draw, or add any other elements to design your stage any way you'd like.

MAKE IT BETTER: WRITE IT OUT

Before you even write a line of computer code, you map out all your instructions in something called **pseudocode**. Pseudocode is a way of writing detailed instructions for a computer, but in easy-to-understand, everyday language. It's the step before writing code in a programming language.

Try writing out the pseudocode for the show you just planned out. Here's an example:

- Band enters from backstage
- Guitar player starts playing song
- Point spotlight at guitar player
- Turn on spotlight

Wow, you are breezing through this book! And believe it or not, you've also learned a whole bunch of coding concepts. Now's a good time to do a quick review of some key words and introduce a few others.

Oh, but you have to find them first!

INPUT: Data or information that is put into a computer to process.

OUTPUT: The product of a computer process.

PROGRAMMING LANGUAGE: A programming language is a set of rules and instructions used to write computer programs. There are many different programming languages that you can use to do different things.

VARIABLES: Variables are like containers that are used in a program to store and remember information. Variables can hold numbers, strings of letters, and even whether something is true or false!

LOOP: Loops are a way of writing one piece of code that repeats multiple times until a new instruction ends the loop.

CONDITIONAL: Conditionals are elements of code that only happen if something else happens. Conditionals are also called if statements, because *if* something is true, then another thing will happen.

ALGORITHM: An algorithm is a set of steps that a computer follows to complete a task.

FUNCTION: A function is a list of steps in a program that are all wrapped up together, like a math problem, or a musical theme.

PSEUDOCODE: A way of writing detailed instructions for an algorithm, but in easy-to-understand, everyday language. You then translate your pseudocode into code with a programming language.

```
S  U  B  B  M  T  N  B  J  Q  M  I  K  C  N  C  G  S  N
E  U  F  F  X  V  F  C  W  I  N  R  Y  S  B  Z  O  G  M
D  X  I  U  L  N  F  I  M  P  A  Z  E  H  Y  V  G  V  Q
O  Z  G  K  N  A  G  F  U  Q  N  L  L  K  A  O  A  Y  A
C  A  P  S  L  C  N  T  U  K  B  U  R  Z  M  C  N  O  U
O  L  Z  R  X  W  T  O  R  A  L  G  O  R  I  T  H  M  A
D  W  B  B  L  H  D  I  I  G  V  N  S  A  F  J  D  X  I
U  Z  Z  T  Z  S  V  R  O  T  H  F  P  I  F  I  A  K  I
E  G  A  U  G  N  A  L  G  N  I  M  M  A  R  G  O  R  P
S  D  H  U  A  V  W  X  T  Y  W  D  V  G  Y  W  U  C  Y
P  J  F  Q  A  J  Q  G  T  T  C  C  N  N  V  A  T  E  E
R  M  D  L  N  B  L  W  N  N  Q  O  T  O  F  Y  P  T  E
G  B  A  L  E  I  K  I  Z  X  A  T  C  M  C  Q  U  B  X
B  B  K  H  B  Y  K  O  O  S  G  P  A  A  T  F  T  Y  A
W  X  B  H  J  P  P  O  O  L  Q  W  W  V  C  J  Y  E  T
```

HELPING OTHERS WITH CODE

Hi again—it's me, Lucy! Yay, it's my turn to tell you why I love coding. It's simple: It's because I like to help people! What are *you* interested in? Animals? The environment? Helping those who are less fortunate? Well, coding is a great way to get involved in whatever cause you care about. I'm interested in health and want to use coding to solve problems for people who are trying to get over an illness or adopt a healthier lifestyle.

What about you? Describe causes you're interested in here.

Draw your favorite cause or issue.

Why is this cause important to you?

How would you like to help?

How do you think coding could help make a difference for this cause?

HOW CAN I HELP?

All these images represent different causes that rely on volunteers, activists, and people who care to help solve a problem, fix an inequality, or change the way things are done to improve a situation. And in every case, coding is a tool that can be put to work to help solve problems, connect people, and create change. Color in the logos!

1.

2.

3.

4.

5.

Are you drawn to websites and/or stories that have intriguing logos? Having a clear and easily recognizable image or logo can help a group or cause identify themselves to supporters and volunteers. The image can represent an idea or service in a single simple picture. That recognition is also important in the digital world, because a strong logo can help make a group's website, apps, and other digital tools stand for something, and also stand out. Think about a website you visit often—does it have a logo that appeals to you and draws you in?

Draw a line to match the image on the previous page to the cause you think it best represents.

ENDANGERED OR RESCUE ANIMALS:

This cause is all about helping animals. They can be wild, exotic endangered species that are hunted for their body parts (like elephants for ivory or baby seals for fur), animals whose habitats are being destroyed, or pets that have been mistreated or abandoned.

CLIMATE/ENVIRONMENT, RENEWABLE ENERGY:

Our environment supports all life on earth. Without clean water, air, and soil, living things cannot survive. That's why it's important to take steps to protect our natural resources. Fighting pollution, documenting and dealing with climate change, and finding more sustainable (meaning able to last a long time) ways of farming and producing goods and materials are all important ways to help preserve the environment.

HEALTHCARE, EXERCISE, AND NUTRITION:

What happens when we get sick? For some, it means going to a doctor and getting the treatment they need. For others, getting access to good, affordable healthcare is a big struggle. The elderly, expectant parents, and very young children have special healthcare needs. What about the food we eat and our access to exercise and a healthy lifestyle? Not everyone can afford fresh nutritious food, and as a result, their heath suffers. People who care about these issues try to solve problems in order to give everyone the chance to be healthy and happy.

EQUAL RIGHTS/SOCIAL JUSTICE:

The goal of Girls Who Code is to make sure there are as many women as men qualified to work in computer science. This is because in many areas of society, not just in the tech industry, men and women do not have the same access to jobs and opportunities. It is an example of the inequality that people of different genders, races, religions, and sexual orientations often face. People interested in this cause try to ensure that our society provides equal opportunities, education, and fair treatment to ALL people.

POVERTY/HOMELESSNESS/REFUGEES:

For many people around the world, the idea of learning to code and embracing technology is a far-off dream. This is because they are dealing with severe poverty, homelessness, or are refugees who have had to leave their homes due to war, political instability, extreme weather conditions, or other dangers. There are many ways concerned groups try to help those in these kinds of difficult circumstances.

Take the quiz to find out more about each of these issues.

1. How many wild animals are killed per year for their body parts, like tusks and fur?

    a) 1,000

    b) 5,000

    c) More than 10,000

2. A single wind turbine can produce enough energy to power up to how many homes?

    a) 300

    b) 50

    c) 100

3. How many Americans live in "food deserts," areas without access to fresh, healthy, affordable food?

    a) More than 1 million

    b) More than 10 million

    c) More than 20 million

4. Women are half of the workforce in the US, but still earn less than men doing the same job at the same experience level. How much less do they earn than men?

    a) 20%

    b) 15%

    c) 10%

5. Refugees are people displaced from their homes by war, famine, poverty, or other dangers. How many people in the world are displaced from their homes?

    a) 1 in 10,000

    b) 1 in 1,000

    c) 1 in 100

What did you find most surprising about the information
in the quiz on the previous page?
How do you think coding could solve some of these problems? Write a
response to some of the issues or facts from the quiz that stood out to you.

FIND A GOOD FIT

There are all kinds of products and services you can make with code. Think about the causes from the previous pages. Then place one or more of them under each column and think about digital products or services that could help these causes. What could be a robot, app, or website? Explain why and what they could do.

ROBOT

APP

WEBSITE

Now pick just one of these ideas and sketch it out in detail.

Ask yourself these brainstorm questions
to help you narrow down your idea.
What cause is it for? What would it do? Why is that needed?
What problem will it solve? Who would use it? How would it work?

IDEA LAB: PERSONA CARDS

What you'll need:
scissors and colored pencils,
crayons, or markers.

We've already talked about **user experience**. But how do you know who will actually be using your products and what they might be looking for? Some designers rely on persona cards to help them figure it out. These cards help designers and developers understand what different people want out of their products or services. Sometimes these persona cards are created after doing in-depth interviews with real people, and sometimes they're compilations of different types of users.

Cut out the cards on the next page. Read their profiles. Then answer the following questions.

1. Which person can't wait to go out and get the latest device?

_____

2. Which person would be most interested in a program for sharing and sorting images?

_____

3. Who needs extra time to learn how a device works and why it's useful?

_____

4. Who would like a timer app that would make your smartphone go into airplane mode at certain times so you don't check it too often?

_____

5. Who wants to be able to use a device that makes learning fun?

_____

6. Who would be interested in modifying or customizing their device?

_____

Mom	Dad
Younger sister	Grandma
Best friend	Dog

Dad's not that interested in tech. He likes doing things the way he's always done them and thinks most devices are just the latest fad. He needs to be convinced a device will actually save time or make things easier.

Mom loves trying out new tech, and she's quite good at it. She's always looking for ways to use technology to keep in touch with her family.

Grandma never thought she'd have so much fun trying new tech. She loves taking digital pictures of her grandkids and is learning how to share them with friends on social media.

Little sister loves to play learning and reading games on her devices, but Mom and Dad keep a close eye on her screen time.

Your pet dog doesn't like it when you're on your phone and ignoring him. He loves to eat and play with you.

Your best friend loves to figure out how things work. It's not enough just to use devices, she wants to figure out how to code them herself.

You know that icons and logos are valuable visual tools to help identify a cause. Now it's your turn to color in or come up with your own icon or logo for the cause *you* are most interested in.

_____   _____

_____   _____

MAKE IT BETTER

Wow, you've done a lot of great thinking about different causes so far! Let's try to put it all together. Pick your favorite persona from your card. Now copy the icons you just made and place them on this blank home screen for a website. Color or draw in any other features or style elements you think your persona would like.

Why did you design this the way you did?

Why did you pick the logo, colors, and style?

How did your persona influence your design?

How do you think this site will help your cause? How can you make it better?

- -

- -

- -

- -

- -

- -

- -

- -

- -

- -

- -

DESIGN LAB: WIRE FRAME YOUR FUNDRAISING APP

What you'll need: scissors and a glue stick.

Annotated wireframes are a way of mapping out how an app will function. I'm creating a fundraising app for a group that raises money for kids with serious illnesses.

I want to make the app easy to use, and I want to make sure the Volunteer Now! button, which links to an online application, is super easy to find. Can you help?

Cut out the wireframe boxes on the next page and arrange them on the home screen. Write in what each element will be and what it will do, like the Volunteer Now! button.

When you are happy with the layout, glue the wireframes in place.

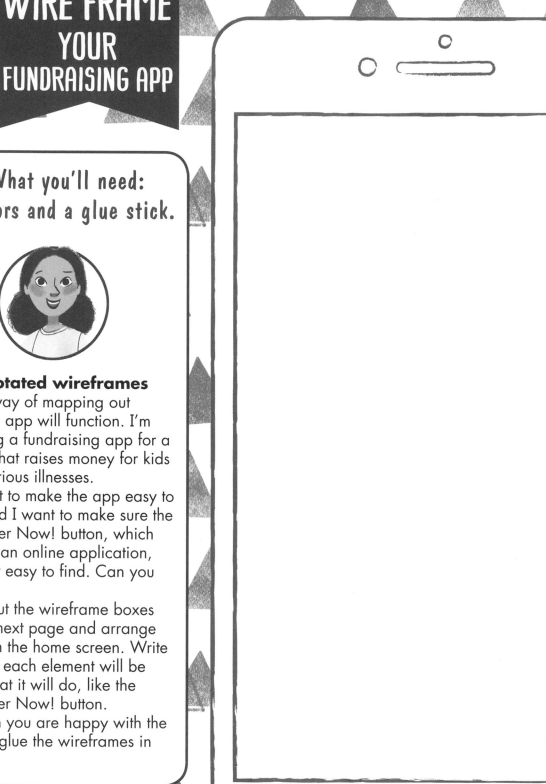

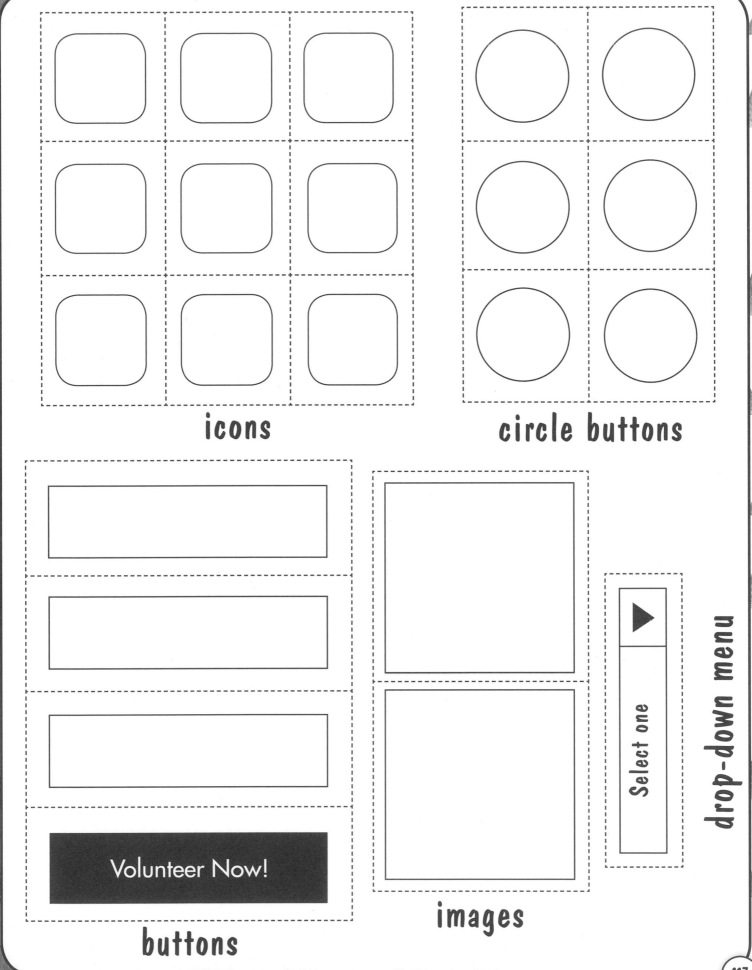

icons

circle buttons

Volunteer Now!

buttons

images

Select one

drop-down menu

117

One last big coding idea we should talk about is **variables**. Variables are like containers that are used in a program to store and remember information—kind of like a pill box for storing vitamins.

Or a craft box for storing art supplies.

Or those big baskets used to store different types of balls and gear in the gym.

Variables are containers that hold contents that can change. In the real world, containers hold vitamins or beads or basketballs. But in coding, variables can hold numbers, strings of letters, and even whether something is true or false! Want to see an example of a collection of changing information or data?

Try out the health and wellness variable exercise on the next page. It's something you need to be ready to do for a week to get a good data set— that means a set of enough observations that you can analyze.

What you'll need: a watch with a second hand or a stopwatch, and drill loop cards.

Start on day one.

Use your watch to take your pulse for sixty seconds. You can find your pulse by placing your first two fingers lightly on the inside of your wrist near your hand.

Count the number of beats in sixty seconds. Note the number in the table.

Then use your drill loop cards to move through a round of exercise.

Then take your pulse again. Note the results. How have they changed?

Repeat for six more days in a row.

Congratulations, you've just created a data set! What do you notice about how your heart rate changes after you exercise? Does your heart rate get faster or slower after exercise? Compared to the beginning of the week, is your heart rate getting as fast at the end of the week?

DATE	PULSE BEFORE EXERCISE	PULSE AFTER EXERCISE	OBSERVATIONS

JOURNAL PAGES

What did you learn that you didn't know before?

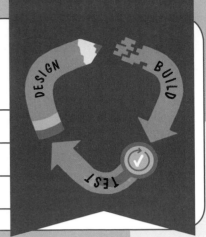

_____

_____

_____

What was your favorite topic in this book?

_____

_____

_____

_____

What was your favorite part of the design build process?

_____

_____

_____

_____

Are you going to start learning to code?

_____

_____

_____

_____

Guess what, you already have!

ANSWER KEY

Page 9

1. True

2. False: While robots may be able to pick up on human emotional cues and select a programmed response, they cannot generate and feel real emotions like humans do—at least not yet. Some researchers predict that eventually artificial intelligence (which is the creation of intelligent machines that can interact like humans) in robots will be able to generate simple emotions.

3. True

4. True

5. False, but in Japan there is a robot that is designed to identify different types of cheese.

6. True

Page 10

C. Exploring Mars

Page 12

A3

B1

C2

Page 15

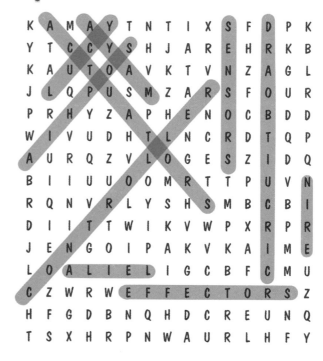

Page 18

Page 32

| | | | | | | | | | | | | | | |
|L|A|P|T|O|P| | |P|A|I|N|T| | |

Crossword answers:
1. LAPTOP
2. PENCIL
3. PALETTE
4. CLAY
5. BRUSH
6. DIGITAL
7. CAMERA
CHALK

Pages 34–35

1. Laptop
2. Digital camera
3. Tablet and digital pen

Page 56

Helmet

Surfboard

T-shirt

Page 62

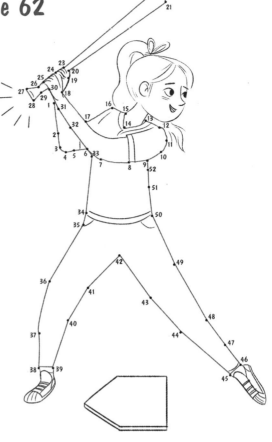

Page 63

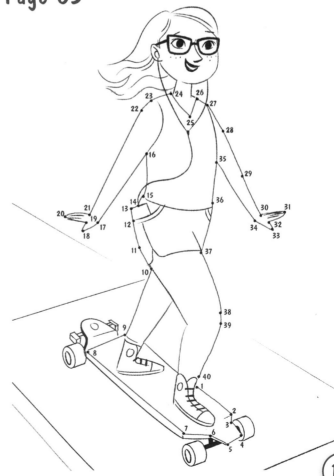

Page 73

- Baseball
- Website
- Track and field
- Stopwatch
- Digital device
- Jump shot
- Penalty
- Racket
- Snowboard
- Helmet camera

Page 87

- Choreography
- Lighting design
- Sound mixing board
- Synthesizer
- Costume
- Director
- Concert
- Performance
- Music
- Theater

Pages 74–75

Page 83

Page 101

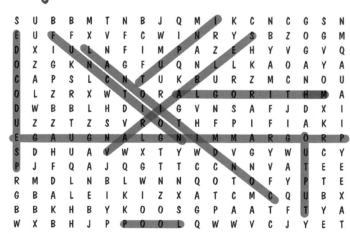

Pages 104–105

1. Healthcare, Exercise, and Nutrition
2. Poverty/Homelessness/Refugees
3. Endangered or Rescue Animals
4. Climate/Enviornment, Renewable Energy
5. Equal Rights/Social Justice

Page 106

1. c
2. a
3. c
4. a
5. c

Pages 110–111

1. Mom
2. Grandma
3. Dad
4. Dog
5. Younger sister
6. Best friend

Page 119

Don't miss these other Girls Who Code books!

A New York Times Best Seller

The Friendship Code

by Stacia Deutsch

from New York Times Best-Selling Author Stacia Deutsch

Team BFF: Race to the Finish!

Lights, Music, Code!

by Jo Whittemore

RESHMA SAUJANI
founder of Girls Who Code and the creator of the national movement to close the gender gap in tech

The instant New York Times bestseller!

LEARN to CODE and CHANGE the WORLD

Code It! Create It!
Ideas + Inspiration for Coding

by Sarah Hutt